MW00953931

Calling All ANGELS

Calling All ANGELS

✦

The Compelling Story of a woman who says, "I have talked to ANGELS, and ANGELS have talked to me."

Prophetess Mary Dickerson

iUniverse, Inc.

New York Lincoln Shanghai

Calling All ANGELS

The Compelling Story of a woman who says, "I have talked to ANGELS, and ANGELS have talked to me."

Copyright © 2006 by Mary Dickerson

All rights reserved. No part of this book may be used or reproduced by any means, graphic, electronic, or mechanical, including photocopying, recording, taping or by any information storage retrieval system without the written permission of the publisher except in the case of brief quotations embodied in critical articles and reviews.

iUniverse books may be ordered through booksellers or by contacting:

iUniverse
2021 Pine Lake Road, Suite 100
Lincoln, NE 68512
www.iuniverse.com
1-800-Authors (1-800-288-4677)

All interior photos courtesy of Rebecca Lewis

ISBN-13: 978-0-595-41728-5 (pbk)
ISBN-13: 978-0-595-86068-5 (ebk)
ISBN-10: 0-595-41728-0 (pbk)
ISBN-10: 0-595-86068-0 (ebk)

Printed in the United States of America

Contents

A Love letter to God

Dear God,

I give you all the praise, for with you, I could have not faced another day. You have been a mother to me when my mother couldn't be a mother. You have been a father to me too, a friend; because my friends are few. You have been and continue to be my strength, hope also my peace in the mist of my many storms. You continue to walk with me on this journey, and it is because of you, I can do all things. Without YOU, I can do nothing.

Lovingly,
Dear Heart

Acknowledgements

First, I wish to thank GOD and his Angels for this experience It has been life changing. I want to thank my Pastor Elder Eugene Lewis Jr. who is also my son, and eldest now that Doug has gone to be with Jesus. I dedicate the second chapter to you, because you were with me when my submission angel came to visit. I wish to thank my husband Hercules Dickerson, because you are my inspiration, and my motivation. Special thanks to my daughter Lisa Lewis; because you are such a risk taker, you have helped me work through my fears. The best to you, you deserve only the best. Also, much love and thanks to Joshua and Alex. Alex follow your dreams because they can come true. Josh push as hard as you can. When you were born, the spirit said, "Call him *Joshua*, for he shall finish your work." Also, my baby boy; Michael. Thanks for all your hard work with this book. Without you, it would have been a tougher task. And last but not least, Rebecca; my baby girl thank, you. You helped me put the finishing touches on a long hard job. I love all of you. You guys are simply the best.

Thank you to the publishers, for all your hard work. You made my dream come true. Special Thanks also to Glamour Shots Photography. You guys are the best. Thanks for capturing the spirit of what I could not have put into words. Also, Anthony and Hook. Thanks for being my sons best friends. You guys will always be like sons to me. To Carl, thanks for not giving up.

And last, but certainly not least, to my son's children. Thanks for giving Doug some sunshine through all of his pain.

The Prophetess, Mary Dickerson

Introduction

My name is Mary Dickerson, and I am a *prophetess*. What is a prophetess you may ask? A prophetess is a woman who receives messages from God; we also receive messages from the Holy Spirit. We warn the people of God; instruct and equip them.

Through my experiences with angels. I hope to encourage our readers to walk with God. In the first part of this book, I will share my experiences with my spiritual warfare angels. I hope you will grasp the importance of using your spiritual warfare angels.

PART I
Spiritual Warfare Angels

There are forces that are working against our walk with God. That's why it is so important that we send our *angels* to fight on our behalf. Because there are forces fighting against us that we can't see with our natural eye, we must use our *spiritual* eye. First *natural*, then *spiritual*. Our spiritual warfare angels also defeat the strong hold of Satan.

We need our spiritual warfare angels, because spiritual wickedness is a stronghold, it can be a road block that slows down our road block with God. Once this road block is removed; we can proceed freely. EVERY believer needs to send these angels to battle. The battle really isn't ours; it's the LORDS. My personal encounter with *my* spiritual warfare began when I had a family crisis. My family was being threatened to be torn apart. My marriage was at risk, kids were being hurt, and my focus was being affected.

I prayed and fasted night and day, I kept believing in the Lord and then; I had a vision, a message, and then the answer to my prayer came. In the first vision, I saw a fleet of angels just waiting and relaxing. They seem to be vacationing. I asked who they were and why they were so at ease. The message I was told was they were my *spiritual warfare angels.* They were at rest because I hadn't given them any work. I asked, "How can I?" Then the Holy Spirit instructed me to speak these words: **"Spiritual Warfare Angels; sick 'em, go get 'em!** Then instantly an angel appeared before me with wings that stretched out in the distance far and wide. He also was carrying a musical instrument. He blew into it, and all of the angels around him came prepared for battle equipped with swords. By the word of God a great legion, an army of angels came out of the mountains. My spiritual warfare angel stood in front of them all. Then the spirit moved me to speak these words again, "**Sick 'em, go get 'em!**" This great angel dropped his instrument, and they were then mounted on horses. They attacked all the spiritual wickedness in my life on my behalf. It rained saw and dust on the earth and I asked, "What is this?" I could hear moaning and groaning in the air. I was told to not worry, it is *done*. The sounds were only the crying before death of the wickedness in my life. This book will make the mystery known of some of the powers we possess in Jesus.

Ephesians 6:13-19 reads, "Wherefore take you the whole <u>amour</u> of God that you may be able to withstand in the evil day, and having done all to stand. **Stand** therefore, having your loins girt about the truth, and having the breastplate of righteousness. **And** your feet shod with the preparation of the gospel of peace; Above all taking the shield of faith, were with you shall be able to quench all the fiery darts of the wicked. **And** take the helmet of salvation and the sword of the spirit. Which is the word of God. Praying always with all prayer and supplication in the spirit, and watching there with all perseverance and supplication for all saints. **And** for me, that utterance may be given to me, that I may open my mouth boldly, to make known the mystery of the gospel."

As a prophetess of the Lord, it is also my responsibility to make known the mysteries of God, and serve as an inspiration to others. The scriptures give evidence. We have angels waiting to help us with our walk with Christ.

As stated in 1Timothy 1:18-19 reads: "This charge I commit to you, son Timothy according to the *prophecies* which went on before you, that you might by them war a good **warfare**. **And** holding faith, and a good conscience, which some having put away concerning faith have been made shipwreck."

Don't live feeling weak and defenseless. We have angels waiting, to help us. But if you don't know this, how can you make use of them? The bible says, "My people perish because lack of knowledge, but be not confused, these angels work on behalf of the Lord Jesus." These angels are employees of Heaven. Be careful, they are working with you, and they are sent by God.

Psalm 91:1-13 reads, "He that dwells in the secret place of the most high shall abide under the shadow of the almighty. **And** I will say of the Lord, he is my refuge, and my fortress. My God in him I will trust. **And** surely he shall deliver you from the snare of the fowler, and from the Noisome Pestilence. **And He** shall cover you with his feathers, and under his **wings** shall you thrust, his truth shall be your shield and buckler. **And** you shall not be afraid for the terror at night, nor for the arrow that flies by day. Nor for the pestilence that walk in darkness, nor for the destruction that wastes at noon day. A thousand shall fall at thy side, and ten thousand at your hand, but it shall not come near you. Only with your eyes shall you behold and see the reward of the wicked. Because you hast made the Lord, which is my refuge. Even the most high, your habitation, There shall no evil befall you, neither shall any plague come near you dwelling. For he shall give his **angels** charge over you, to keep you in all your ways. They shall bear you up in their hands, lest you dash your foot against a stone. You shall tread upon the lion and adder; the young lion and dragon shall trample under your feet."

Read these scriptures daily to help yourself to become stronger in Lord. Isaiah 54:17 is especially important. It says, "No weapon that is formed against you shall prosper, and every tongue that shall rise against you in judgment, you shall condemn. This is the heritage of the servants of the Lord, and their righteousness is of me, says the Lord." This is our God given right we have inherited this promise by the prophet Isaiah. Psalm 35:5 "Let them be as chaff before the wind, and let the Angel of the Lord **chase** them. Let their way be dark and slippery, let the Angels of the Lord persecute them."

Our spiritual warfare angels are ready to do battle on our behalf. You have to send for them. These scriptures reaffirm my experiences. They are all found in the King James version of the bible. I know that I am no longer in bondage. I am FREE. I am no longer a slave; I am free.

Colossians1:26 say, "Even the **mystery** which has been hidden from ages and from generations, but now is made *manifest* to his saints. In the book of Revelation12:7 and war was in heaven, Michael and his Angels fought against the dragon. The dragon fought with his angels. And prevailed not, neither was their place found anymore in heaven."

Verse 9 says, "And the great dragon was cast out, that old serpent called the Devil and Satan, which deceives the whole world; he was cast out into the earth." So were his angels. When the enemy was cast out of Heaven, he became angry. He lost before, and he will lose again. Now you and I have taken another step toward our destiny. Now stand up and send your Spiritual Warfare Angels to fight for you. We must send our Spiritual Warfare Angels to fight for us.

Repeat these words; "Spiritual Warfare Angels, I send you now to fight on my behalf to defeat evil in my life; to break any generational curse in my family, and to burst every bond, break every yoke, and to set the captive free. In Jesus name I pray. **Go now. Sick em' Go get em'!**

PART II
The Family Angel and Submitting Yourself

This chapter exposes the fact that we all want to be in control, when in reality, two headed things are abnormal. What does a two headed thing desire above all? *Separation.* My experiences with my Family Angel gave me this revelation. If you are having a family or relationship problem, it could be because you are not submitting yourself to each other. I used to associate submission with weakness. In reality, it is very powerful.

My experiences began in the mist of a family crisis. The pain and burden of it all had me in deep despair. One day I called my son/pastor Eugene for help. So, he came over to my house, and we began to pray in the spirit. It was a very powerful experience. We prayed so much, that I began to see an angel. He in the appeared in the kitchen! I didn't say anything to my pastor, but guess what; he saw the angel also! My *family angel* remained in my home for at least 2 weeks, maybe longer. My family angel taught me how to submit myself to my husband. After work everyday, when I went home I would get in the bed and pray. Then one day I was told I had to give *birth* to submission. I had physical pain in my stomach similar to labor, until it was birthed! I felt relieved. I can't explain what I really felt. I will simply say, I felt *changed.* Even my co-workers noticed a physical change in me.

My family angel never left the kitchen while he was in my home. I asked my submission or family angel, "How long will you be here?" and he replied "Until the man comes home." He was referring to my husband who had left our home at the time. One day my oldest daughter Lisa was in the kitchen talking on the phone. I could tell by her conversation, that she was talking to the man in her life that had been giving her a lot of grief. Then suddenly after she hung up the phone, my family angel touched her on her shoulder! She screamed, "Who did that!" I asked her what happened. She said that she had felt someone touch her. I didn't want her to be frightened, so I told her about my family angel in the kitchen. She asked me how long he had been there, and when was he going to leave. I told her that he had been here for over a week, and he said he was going to stay until your dad comes home. We hugged each other and cried. And with the touch she received from my family angel, she began to get over her bad relationship, and now it's completely over! I later on redecorated my kitchen, and dedicated it to my family Angel. The back slogan of my kitchen was "We believe in Angels." I filled the kitchen with Angel pictures and put Angel figurines on each side of the window seal. Even though we have since moved, I will always have fond memories of my Family Angel.

One day my family angel asked me a question. It was; "In what order do you put, your relationship with God, family, and your husband"? I told him that I relied on my husband first, then my relationship with God, and then the children. I was told that the order was wrong, and should be changed. He told me GOD had to be first, then husband, then children. Now that my order has changed, my peace has been restored. Now I will never let anything separate me from God. Not even my husband, or my children. NOTHING. God is my first love, and when I put my life in the correct order, that is subject. I submit myself to God, my husband, and we must be subject one to the other. That is the order of God.

Romans 13, verse 1 reads: "Let every souls be subject to the higher powers, for there is no power but of God, the powers that be are ordained from God." Notice the word **power** is used more than once in that scripture.

You see, being subject has been misunderstood. Some of us misinterpret subject as being weak. Which is a trick of Satan. Being subject is powerful!

Romans 13 verses 2-3 reads "whosoever therefore resists the power resists the ordinance of God, and they that resist, shall receive to themselves, damnation." You see, resist means not being subject. Verse 3: "For rulers who are not a terror to good works, but to evil will then not be afraid of power? Do that which is good and you shall have the praise of the same." Notice there is a question asked; will you be afraid of the power?

If you haven't learned submission, because you are afraid of being hurt and used, we must not resist it. We are fighting the power of submission, and we must *not* resist it.

I was asked to preach at my church one Sunday. This is something I do on a regular basis. But I myself was still going through my own trial. My husband was still gone away from the family. I knew I had to do God's work, so I prayed, fasted, and I went. There was also a lady at my church who was going through a trial similar to mine. Her husband was gone as well. The spirit of the Lord told me to pray for her. And as I did, I received a revelation of men all over the world leaving their families, or have already left. The spirit called these men *home*. All of the men from the North, South, East and West. With names from A-Z. So, I sent my family angel to help.

Everyone send your family angels to help as I did. I saw women in the spirit who needed to learn to be the subject or submit to their husband. For it was a trick of the enemy to drive these men out of these homes and break up families. The enemy will then destroy the family. He will send bitterness to these women. The children will go astray, and the evil works will be done. This is a prophesy, and after I preached this message at my church that Sunday, and the prophesy was done, I proclaimed I required my husband to be saved, and returned to home to his family.

Days went by, and suddenly in the spirit, I heard "Take it back." I heard this twice. I asked "Take back what?" And the voice said, "What you said about your husband being saved, and returning home." I replied, "No, I will NOT!" The evil spirit said my husband won't EVER return home. I said, "So be it, but I will NOT take it back!"

That night the enemy attacked my dreams. I dreamed of my husband with other women. But I still refused to take it back.

One morning I was getting ready for work, and I went in the kitchen to catch a glimpse of my family angel. He had changed clothes! I thought this was odd. But what I didn't know was that he was *leaving*. I said, "But you told me you would stay until my husband came home, and he's still gone." My family angel told me, "It's a shift change. You don't need me anymore." He then suddenly left.

I was stunned. I went to work troubled in my spirit all day. I came home after work, fell upon my bed and cried. I hadn't wanted him to leave. Then the phone rang. It was my youngest daughter Rebecca. I knew she was sick, I had to pick her up from work a couple days before.

She said, "Dad just called me, and he wants to come home. He wants me to pick him up." I said, "Are you kidding?" She began to cry, and said, "No Mom, It's true." Then she got out of bed and went to pick him up. She ran in the house ahead of him and said to me, "Mom, please don't be mad at him." I told her I wouldn't. This was a week before Christmas. We were all together for Christmas! And that lady at my church who I prayed for who's husband was gone also, he's home too!

1 Peter 3-22 reads: "He who is gone into heaven, and is on the right hand of God, angels, authorities and powers being made subject to him." Even Jesus was subject, and now that he is on the right hand of authority and power, they are made subject to him. You see, when we are subject to God and one another, we receive power. That's a revelation, to be powerful. **Learn submission.**

1 Peter 5:5: Likewise, you younger submit yourself to the elder, yea all of you be subject to one another, and be clothed with humility for God resists the proud, and gives grace to the humble." We need to put on submission, and wear it like a garment. God will embrace us, and give his grace and his favors.

Luke 22:42 says "Father if you be willing remove this cup from me, nevertheless not my will, but yours be done. Verse43: "And there *appeared an angel* to him from heaven, who strengthened him."

Notice Jesus' statement in verse42 about submitting himself to God. And also notice an **angel** appeared after the submission to God. He could fulfill his destiny now. Submission is powerful, and will get God's attention. It will get you help, in your time of need.

Say this prayer: "Lord Jesus I submit myself to you, and those over me. I ask for help. If it's a generation curse, I ask you to remove it from my family now. In Jesus' name I pray, AMEN."

This is a picture of the house I lived in where I had my angel visits. I was hurt when we sold it because I didn't think I would see them ever again.

PART III
Prosperity Angel

The purpose of this book is to share my experiences and to help others. It is help you get a better understanding of the importance of your life experiences. In this chapter, you will learn how to open your prosperity gate, and how to activate your wealth.

Now I will share my experiences with my prosperity angel. One day after returning home from the mailbox, and receiving yet another stack of bills, my spirit became vexed. Suddenly these words came out of my mouth. "Prosperity Angel, bring prosperity, NOW!" I felt these words had affected me, so I continued to say them. Later on that day, I had a vision of my *Prosperity Angel*. I learned that I needed the keys to prosperity, and here are the words I was told to say: "Prosperity angel, bind poverty in my life, and loose prosperity, NOW!" For the bible says, "Whatsoever we bind in the earth, we also bind in heaven, and whatsoever we loose in this earth, we also loose in heaven."

Days later, I had another vision. I was standing in front of a large gate. I could see *hands* pulling at the lock, and I could hear voices crying. "What does this mean? I asked. Prosperity angel told me that they were my requests shaking the gate. I couldn't get in. Prosperity angel appeared on the right side of me. He stood about 7 feet tall, wore gold garments, and held a staff in his hand. And then he *spoke through me* these words: "OPEN THE GATE."

After I said that, I asked him "Why did you speak through me?" He replied, "Because I am the gate keeper, and you are the owner." The gate began to slide open. I saw gold, silver, money, and large amounts of something that I cannot describe. He said, "GO IN." I went inside and I said "Wow, this is wonderful!" I was jumping around and smiling. Then I left. But I was troubled in my spirit still. Prosperity Angel asked me, "What did you get when you went in?" "Oh no, I didn't get *anything.*" Why didn't I bring any of the wealth out with me? So I began to pray. If you are like most of us, you get credit card offers in the mail. They only work after you *activate* the card.

So I was given these words. "Prosperity angel, bind poverty for 50 years now!" "Prosperity Angel loose prosperity for 50 years now!" John 3:2 says, "Beloved, I wish above all things that you may prosper, and be in health, even as your soul prospers." Get an understanding of this scripture. The wealth of our soul, and the prosperity of our life, should be of equal value. Do inventory of the wealth of your soul, and the wealth you actually posses is what makes us poor. It's bad credibility. Let's break down the word *credibility.* The first word is *credit.* How is your credit? If it is bad, there is a trust issue. If we are not trustworthy, we are considered dishonest. Need I say more? Be honest and trustworthy. This will increase your souls value. Don't be covetous. Stop trying to get something like someone else's. Stop wishing for someone else's lifestyle.

Read Deuteronomy 8:11-18. "Forget, not the lord your God in not keeping his commandments, and his judgment and his statutes, which I command you this day. **VERSE 12** "Lest when you have eaten and are full, have built godly houses, and dwelled therein." **V13** "**And** when your herds flock multiply, silver and gold is multiplied." **V14** "Then your heart be lifted up, and you forget the lord your God, which brought you forth out of the land of Egypt, from the house of bondage." **V15** "Who lead you through that great and terrible wickedness? Where are fiery serpents, scorpions drought, while there was no water. Who brought you forth water out of the rock of flint?"

Don't forget **God**, when your wealth comes.

Deuteronomy 11:16, "Who fed you in the wilderness with the manna, which your fathers knew not he might humble you, and that he might prove you to do you good at your latter end. And you say in your heart, my power and the might of my hand has gotten me this wealth." So be very careful that you don't try to get credit for the wealth that you have obtained. The glory belongs to God.

I would like to share a scripture with you. 2 Chronicles:20. "And they rose early in the morning, and went forth into the wilderness of Te'koa: and as they went forth, Jehosh' a-plat, stood and said, "Hear me O' Judah, and your inhabitants of Jerusalem; believe in the Lord your God, so shall you be established. Believe his *prophets*, and you shall prosper."

This scripture contains a revelation. Believing in his prophet, and I am a prophetess. Faith without work is dead. If you mediate on these revelations, your wealth will come true. Be careful that you don't try to get the credit for the wealth you have obtained. Let the glory be to God.

Deuteronomy 8;18 says, "But you shall remember the Lord your God, for it is He that gives you the **power to get wealth,** that he may establish his covenant, which he swore to your fathers, as it is this day.

Proverbs 13:11 says, "Wealth gotten by vanity shall be diminished: but he that gathers by labor shall increase."

All these scriptures are given to increase your faith. Because of my experiences with prosperity angel, I am now debt free. I have purchased TWO new cars which my husband and I OWN. May God richly bless all of you. To God be the Glory!

Prosperity Angel is teaching me how to obtain wealth. He has instructed me to start a business, which I am working on while I am writing this book. Also, this book was his idea! Prosperity angel also teaching me how to invest my earnings, he's very wise. The rest is left up to my *Destiny* angel. He was with me for my book cover shot, it was his idea. And now I dance with my Destiny, and so can you.

At the end of my encounter with my Prosperity Angel, I witnessed a meeting. I saw my Spiritual Warfare, Family, and Prosperity Angels talking to my *Destiny* Angel. I knew it was time for me to call for my Destiny Angel. I learned a lot from *all* of the angels. My Spiritual Warfare Angel made this journey passable by removing all my obstacles. My Family Angel taught me how to be a powerful and obedient woman of God, and to protect my Family. My Prosperity Angel gave me the keys to unlock my future wealth. And Now I am dancing with my Destiny Angel, and I am anxiously waiting to see what he has in store for me.

This is my car BEFORE prosperity angel did the works for me in my life. I decided to keep it. I'll always remember what my prosperity angle did for me.

Here's my new BMW! My 740IL is fully loaded, including bullet proof glass, a mobile phone, and cable T.V. I named her *Prosperity Angel (which is also on my license plate cover*) in honor of my angel who visited me. It's also paid for in cash. I am very blessed. Thanks Prosperity Angel!

This is the car my husband was driving BEFORE my prosperity angel came to visit. I later on donated it to the kidney foundation, in memory of my son.

My husband Hercules (pictured) owns this 740I sports edition, fully loaded, which drives like a dream. His personal license plate cover reads "Da Whip," which is a nickname he calls his car.

PART IV

Dancing with My Destiny

Destiny speaks; he beckoned for me, and I see myself dancing with my *Destiny* partner. He's swinging me around, as we dance down the path of a winding highway. Then one day out of the blue, he gives me a vision. I see a man driving down the highway. The road comes to a dead end. He gets out of the car, and sits on the hood. He loosens his shirt collar, and holds his head into his hands. And Destiny asks me, "What shall he do?" Before I could answer, I noticed another car parked next to him. There were clothes all over the inside. It looked as though it had been lived in. Then as I began to answer, "Maybe they should turn around." Destiny said, "This is your life, you can't start all over again." He said, "Many have come to a dead end, and if it happens to you, remember this: The man and the people are stuck because they are trying to take people with them on their destiny trip, who can NOT go. They are trying to figure out a way, but there is no way. THEY CAN NOT GO.

The bible says, "Take up our cross, and follow him." If we refuse, we will be stuck at a dead end. This can not be CHANGED!

I began writing this book through a lot of pain and family problems. My husband tells me he wants to sell our home. My head says, NO WAY, but my submission angel says YES! So I reluctantly agreed. Before we sold the house, I had sadness in my heart. You see, I had my angel visits in *this* house. Now facing the possibility of leaving them, I was very sorrowful.

But life goes on. Lots of things began to unfold before the house was even sold. My oldest son, who is also my best friend, has been diagnosed with Renal Failure for well over 10 years. I had tried to give him one of *my* kidneys, but his hypertension would always postpone the surgery.

Before we even got a FOR SALE sign in the yard, we had two offers on the table. Our house was sold within a few weeks. Then out of the blue, my son was rushed to the hospital, and placed in ICU. After a few days of treatment, the Doctor told me that he had done all he could do. My son died within a two week period. Since we had accepted the offer for our house the previous week, and my son had died the following week, we were moving and planning a funeral, all at the same time.

I had an angel visit with Dougie while he was in the hospital. I was told these words; "Give him back to me. I don't want to take him from you, so give him back." I replied, "No, I can't!" But I was strengthened and was finally able to say the hardest words I have ever spoken. I then said, "I give him back." I repeated these words two or three times, through tears and pain. I whispered into Dougie's ears these words: "If you choose to go, don't worry about me, I won't be mad at you for leaving. But if you choose to stay, I will fight for you with God's angels, and all that I have within me. I love you. He was not able to speak, (he had been incoherent for days now) I whispered to him that he could still talk to God using your mind. He reads minds. I love you" I began to cry and I turned my head because I didn't want him to worry about me. And then he said, "I LOVE YOU." This was the first time he had spoken since he had been in ICU. I knew he had heard me!

As I left the hospital that night, I *knew* that I had to give my son back to Jesus. I was having such a hard time doing this. I was crying so hard that I could barely see the road driving home. So I said,

"Angels take me home I can hardly see." My husband Hercules was following me home in his car right behind me. He had come to the hospital straight from work. And suddenly I had another vision. This time it was of my son's oldest child Doug Jr. You see, he died when he was just a little boy. I could see him! He was all grown up, and was about 18 or 19 years old. He was standing on what looked like the edge of heaven. There were 2 *angels* on each side of him. Then he leaned forward, cupped his hands around his mouth yelled as loud as he could: "DAD! DAD!" I began to shake my head and waved my hands at him telling him to stop. I could see my son looking in his direction, and I knew he wanted to go. But I was still holding on to him And then one of his angels said "Let him come to be with his son, for we have raised him already." That's when I knew I had to let him go.

I believe if I hadn't had these angel visits, I could not have made it though these tough obstacles in my life. My family and I have moved to our new place. Recently, I just had my first Mother's Day without my son Dougie. We visited his grave site that day, and gave I him flowers. He was always giving gifts to me, and on this day I decided to give him a gift for all the gifts he had given me over the years. He was such a great gift giver.

On my first birthday without him, I was filled with such sadness and pain. In our family, he was always the first one to wish me a happy birthday. He made it a game among his bothers and sisters. So I was missing him a lot that day. But he did *visit* me as I was getting ready for work. The window blinds began to move back and forth. I checked to see if they were open, but they weren't. "You beat the other kids again," I said. I felt better because I knew he was missing me, just as much as I was missing him.

"Dougie, since you left, there is a hole in my heart, and it's like a puzzle with one piece missing. Mothers will understand this. But I believe that you are in the arms of the angels. I love you."

This is my son Dougie who went on to be with Jesus. He was not only my son, but my best friend. He will always have a special place in my heart.

This is a picture taken the day of my son's funeral. The motorcycle club shown is my God son's. He was one of my son's best friends, and his motorcycle club escorted my son to the burial site. They are called the "Soul Brothers."

Here's a picture of me taken the day on my son's funeral. I have always wanted to learn how to ride a motorcycle, and on this day my God son "Hook", (right) let me take a picture with HIS motorcycle.

◆   ◆   ◆

A few months later, my family and I were taking pictures of our cars. We took a picture of our oldest daughter's car. After the photos were developed, we noticed a ring around the photo of her car. Everyone in my family was trying to figure out exactly what, and how exactly this ring appeared around her car. This ring hadn't been on any of the other pictures. I told my family these were her angels all around her car. A few weeks later, my oldest daughter Lisa and I were on our way to the store. We were involved in a terrible accident. We were rear ended by a pick up truck, knocked into an SUV. We ran over the sidewalk into some small trees and landed near a deep embankment. We were resting just inches from the edge. I called 911 from my cell phone immediately. My daughter had to be cut from the car, using the Jaws of Life. I was wearing a pair of small angel wings around my neck that she had given me for Mother's Day. When she was removed from the car by the Fire. Department, the necklace was lying on the seat. She saw it, and asked one of the firefighters to give it to her. She called to me as she was laying on the stretcher and handed it to me. I touched my neck. I didn't even know it was off! And guess what. It wasn't broken! The clasp had came open! The angels held the car up! There was a wash to the left of the embankment, but we did not go over. We are fine. No broken bones and we are ALIVE. To God be the Glory!

This is a picture of my daughters' car, which was taken before the accident. Notice the ring around the car? I believe these were her Angels who protected us from being hurt in or killed. The beam of light that is coming down over the door, is right where my daughter was trapped! To God Be the Glory!

My life up until now has always been filled with pan and despair. But now, I have a better understanding of my struggle, it kept me close to the Lord, because there was no one else to lean on. And I am not bitter because of my life struggle. I am *better* because of it.

I encourage you to call on your angels. Make sure you have finished your purpose with each of them, before you move on to the next. And because I did, I was told purpose and destiny shook hands.

I hope my story will stir my readers up to fulfill *their* purpose in life, and to dance with their Destiny Angel, as have I.

978-0-595-41728-5
0-595-41728-0

Made in the USA
Las Vegas, NV
06 May 2022

48473043R00031